T0196330

Talking About Writing

Part Five

A sequential programme of sentence structure, grammar, usage and punctuation for grade 12

with accompanying *Answer Key*

"A little learning is a dangerous thing;"
(Alexander Pope, *Essay on Criticism*)

Let's drink more deeply of the Pierian spring.

Shirley Campbell, B.A., M.A.

Acknowledgements

Special thanks to Karl Bensmiller, *Computer Solutions Specialists*
Armstrong, British Columbia

and to Ernie Sollid, Computer Coordinator
School District 83, British Columbia

Order this book online at www.trafford.com
or email orders@trafford.com

Most Trafford titles are also available at major online book retailers.

Print information available on the last page.

ISBN: 978-1-5521-2249-5 (sc)

Trafford rev. 01/17/2023

 www.trafford.com

North America & international
toll-free: 844-688-6899 (USA & Canada)
fax: 812 355 4082

Introduction

Talking about Writing is for high school teachers and students who

    I. need a common vocabulary with which to discuss written language;

    2. desire a working knowledge of the chief elements of sentence structure, grammar, usage and punctuation as they apply to the writing process;

    3. demand an integrated approach, and a sequenced format adaptable to individual lessons; and

    4. appreciate the help of an *Answer Key*.

A mechanic immersed in the intricacies of engine repair does not ask for a "thingummy" or a "whatsit." He or she names the tool and holds out a hand to receive it.

In the same way, teachers and students poring over the products of the writing process need **a basic common vocabulary** with which to discuss the work. They need to make mutually understandable statements which will clarify and improve the material under review. For example, "This sentence contains a misplaced modifier" is more helpful and precise than "Don't you think putting this bit in a different place will make the sentence sound better?" *Talking about Writing* supplies this basic vocabulary.

The text has a simple format. It teaches the recognition of the **nine sentence errors** which writers commonly make. **It integrates the grammar** necessary to understand each sentence error. **Sentence combining, usage, and punctuation exercises** strengthen writing technique.

Talking about Writing fills a need for both a concrete objective in English language study and **a teaching plan**. It provides a method of entry - the nine sentence errors - which is useful to many: beginning teachers, for example; teachers of other subjects who have been asked to pick up one or two blocks of English in the timetable; teachers who wish a clear explanation of the language in the writing process; or parents who run **home school**.

A further advantage is to **make a connection between the teaching of English language and other languages**; such as, French or Spanish. Students studying a second language are expected to recognize, for example, a direct object or a past participle in order to make the necessary agreement. The grammar component accompanying each sentence error encourages the transfer of this knowledge from one language to another.

Talking about Writing **is sequenced and self-explanatory**. In each chapter the material progresses in simple and logical increments to the desired end; namely, to recognize a sentence error in order to discuss written work, practise effective writing techniques, and empower communication. The sentence errors progress in difficulty from grades 8 to 12. **The format is adapted for individual lessons**.

Curriculum guides tend to be written in generalities. *Talking about Writing* **provides the teacher with a pattern**. Having experienced the focus of this programme and the integration of the topics, he or she then knows how to access additional material to suit a student's individual needs.

How *Talking about Writing* is Organized

Students are taught to recognize the nine major sentence errors: two in each of grades 8 to 11, and one in grade 12, as follows:

Grade 8 -   Run-on Sentence
            Sentence Fragment

Grade 9 -   Lack of Parallel Structure
            Misplaced Modifier

Grade 10 -   Dangling Participle
            Lack of Agreement

Grade 11 -   Indefinite Antecedent
            Incorrect Tense

Grade 12 -   Wordiness

The grammar necessary to understand the sentence error is integrated with appropriate punctuation and sentence combining techniques.

A pre-test and a post-test accompany each sentence error, and exercises accompany the grammatical explanation.

A usage section is included for grades 8, 9, and 10, and a review of punctuation for grade 11.

The unit for grade 12 includes instruction on writing forcefully as well as supplementary exercises on the topics learned in grades 8 to 12.

The grade levels are colour coded for accessibility and interest.

How to Use *Talking about Writing*

This text is intended to provide a **finite amount of essential information** for the designated grade. There is light at the end of the tunnel.

In contrast to the leisurely musing which characterizes the composing process, or the angular discussion which accompanies literary analysis, **the pace of a language class is rapid**. Two to five minutes is adequate for a short Practice Exercise. It is left brain activity. Students are learning how to **organize and sharpen** their written work. So the teacher is encouraged to push forward quickly - not a wasted minute. 'Down time' encourages boredom. Keep the class at a gallop.

Language study is fun. **Every exercise is a puzzle**. Encourage the students to play with the concepts. Be patient with 'wrong' answers. Support inquisitiveness. Allow for possibility. If students come away with some knowledge of the intricacies of the language, and some respect for the ways it may be shaped, then the class has achieved its objective.

Students may mark their own or others' work. The overhead projector may be used to demonstrate in sequence the various 'jobs' requested in the Practice Exercises; for example, underline, circle, and draw arrows. Each 'job' may be given one mark and then the Practice Exercise scaled down by division to a reasonable worth. Encourage neatness and the use of a ruler.

At the conclusion of each sentence structure, grammar, or punctuation topic, students are asked to memorize certain aspects and to write definitions in their notebooks. In this way they keep their own record of what they have practised and have study material for tests.

Table of Contents for Grades 8 to 12 Programme

The *Answer Key* to chapters one to fifteen of ***Talking about Writing*** is available as a separate text.

Chapter Thirteen

Grade 12

Wordiness

I. Pre-test on Wordiness

Rewrite concisely the following sentences.

1. My mother and her friends are always exchanging recipes with each other.
2. One important essential in job hunting is a complete resume of one's qualifications and experience.
3. Most modern cars of today carry a radio as part of their standard supply of accessories.
4. Garage sales are a favoured form of buying and selling because the manner in which the items change hands provides a personal touch which perfectly boxed brand name items do not carry, even at the height of intensity provided by $1.49 day at a large department store, which most people have participated in at one time or another.
5. The road was slippery; this was due to the fact that the temperature of the air had dropped to below freezing just after a light rain had fallen on the pavement.
6. My field of endeavour is that of research.
7. Driving the truck into the narrow lane was a mistake because there was no room to turn around once the truck was in the lane, there were large rocks lying in wait to gouge the tires, and the grass was too long at the side of the road to enable the driver to discern whether a ditch was hiding under the grass or not, not to mention the fact that there were cars ahead trying to come out of the lane and other cars behind trying to get in.
8. One main reason why there are so few fish caught in these lakes is because of pollution by mills in the area.
9. With respect to the question of eating at a fast food outlet or a fancy restaurant, I prefer my own kitchen best.
10. I get up at seven-thirty every morning although my alarm goes off at seven but I ignore it, make my bed, brush my teeth, have a shower, fix my hair, eat breakfast, usually just cereal, put the dishes in the sink, collect my books and binders if I can find them, put on my jacket, and walk if I can, or run if I must, down to the bus that is coming to take me to my daily tribulation - school.
11. If you were given a choice between eating fried food or eating baked food, what would it be?
12. It is essential that everybody on this team go all out when we are at practice or when we have a game.
13. Try to find your green slacks, and if you can't, you will have to wait until I get your good ones back from the cleaners.
14. They feel, and I am sure that other people feel the same way about it that they do, that the answer to our problem is not so difficult as we are all making it out to be.
15. Only three women of the original five female Dionne quintuplets are still alive; the others have passed away.

II. Definition of Wordiness

Wordiness is the loss of both sense and force in a sentence because of the failure to state concisely what is meant.

III. Types of Wordiness
A. Overcrowding a sentence with unimportant details

Example:

> • When we entered the theatre, we discovered that it used to be an old opera house, on account of the boxes above the regular rows of seating to the left and right of the stage that it was easy to imagine once held important guests.

Simplify:

> • The boxes to the left and right of the stage indicated to us that the building had once been an opera house.

Practice Exercise 1
Decide which details in the following sentences are unimportant and rewrite the sentences.

1. The mechanic sauntered into the garage at around eight o'clock in the morning, unlocked the till which he had locked up himself the night before, opened a box which he had brought with him from home, and put some change and paper money in the till to get ready for the first customer of the day.
2. Around the first week of September, for five days the town of Armstrong, which is located in the Okanagan Valley in the interior of British Columbia about six hours' drive from Vancouver, is the site of a large agricultural fair which is called the Interior Provincial Exhibition, which is the largest agricultural fair in British Columbia.
3. The owners of a local harness shop, besides making harness and purses and various other leather goods, samples of which hang in the window and make the shop a very interesting place, also fix boots and shoes, which is very lucky because the only shoemaker in town moved to Enderby, which really isn't a long distance to go, being only ten kilometres, but still somewhat of a nuisance.
4. Another interesting shop is the Book Exchange, which is a new shop in town and carries thousands of second-hand books which may be either bought and paid for as a normal book is in a bookstore or exchanged by giving two books for one, any kind of book being accepted, including adventure, romance, western, science fiction, and magazines of all sorts.
5. I think that the fall definitely does have the edge on the other seasons, not even excluding spring, which is usually so welcome after a long, hard winter, because in the fall there is the lovely feeling of just plain relaxation in those days when the sun is still warm and the colours of the trees are so interesting, being red and yellow and purple and brown.

B. Repeating in different words the same thought

Example: • *In my opinion* chocolate brownies are *I feel* the most delicious dessert.

Simplify:
        • Chocolate brownies are my favourite dessert.

Practice Exercise 2
Decide which expressions are redundant and rewrite the sentences.

1. Brown Owl was contented and satisfied with the help and assistance she received from the Pack.
2. She is a good singer as far as having a good voice goes, but she needs direction and guidance in planning and organizing her repertoire of songs.
3. When I returned home again, my family gave me such a hug and squeeze that I thought I was going to be strangled to death.
4. Her friends were pleased and delighted to hear that she had been granted a patent on her new invention.
5. The dogs had the usual habit of roaming about the streets instead of vigilantly guarding the premises.
6. One type of person that I find it hard to hold a conversation with likes to monopolize the entire conversation.
7. After he had written the autobiography of his life, he really had nothing more to say.
8. Having taken part in a marathon of long-distance running, the competitors were totally exhausted and tremendously winded.
9. The average Canadian is no longer amazed or even surprised to hear of multiple births; such as, seven septuplets.
10. Milk is not the universal panacea for the healthy development of infants and babies, since many children are known to have allergic reactions and serious side effects from drinking milk.
11. They had no idea at all of the trials and tribulations that were awaiting the entire team.
12. Several contemporary Canadian poets of our own times have also achieved both fame and renown in countries other than their own.
13. Other places that are favourites to visit in Mexico are the coastal towns lying on the scenic Pacific Ocean due to the fact that water locales hold a special attraction for tourists and other out-of-town visitors.
14. A special feature of the local bi-weekly paper was the *Sports Report* that came out twice a week and covered all the sports activities in the area that week.
15. The barking of the dog recurred again and again to the dismay of the next door neighbours, who begged and pleaded with the owners to make the dog cease and desist from his vociferous and noisy behaviour.

C. Using elaborate or lengthy expressions

Example: • *In the event* of his arriving home late, we shall leave on a light.

Simplify: • *If* he arrives home late, we shall leave on a light.

Practice Exercise 3
Rewrite concisely the following sentences.

1. We were undecided as to whether we should go to the dance or stay home and study for the test.
2. The salesperson said that he liked this brand equally as well as the other one.
3. The effect of so much rain was that it brought about the necessity to build a warehouse to protect the goods from moisture.
4. The question as to whether damages will be assessed in this case is still in the hands of the court.
5. In view of the fact that you will be writing major examinations shortly, it is inadvisable for you to accept a part-time job.
6. There is no doubt but that those same rumours have damaged his chances for achieving political office.
7. These photographs will be used for publicity purposes in the upcoming issue.
8. In the course of the race, the skier favoured for first place missed a turn and dropped back to third spot.
9. The fact that he had gone to trade school was a source of great pride to his parents.
10. At this point in time, we are not able to give you an answer one way or the other.
11. We wish to take this opportunity to reiterate once more the pride and satisfaction we feel in cutting the ribbon on this world-class facility.
12. The low attendance on the part of the public was due to the fact that inclement weather and a modified publicity budget hampered the turn-out.
13. It is incumbent on the chairperson to focus the energies of the group on their main goals.
14. Despite the fact that the dog was clearly terrified of the fire, the intrepid beast retraced its steps again and again to the burning house, now entirely consumed in flames.
15. I can say with complete assurance that this imposing edifice will be ready for occupancy before the first snow flies this fall.
16. She tended to put things off until the last minute and was late every time.
17. He shoes horses for a living and does very well for himself at it.
18. The second to last movie made in the last month of the year about aliens and other life forms was the one that won several awards.
19. In view of the fact that we have only a small amount of firewood left, we need to organize ourselves to get some more.
20. At this point in time, we can safely say that we will meet the deadline.

IV. Post-test on Wordiness
Rewrite concisely the following sentences.

1. There are great numbers of pheasants that abound in these woods.
2. A unique aspect of this design is that it includes safety features which no other similar product of its kind possesses.
3. In order to get ready to leave for camp, he packed shirts, pants, socks, underwear, a jacket, swimming trunks, and a towel, as well as a camera and playing cards, not forgetting his razor and toothbrush, as he had just started to shave and occasionally remembered to brush his teeth - no floss, though, as flossing would have been just too much either to plan for or to endure.
4. Crafts, as well as being an expression of human personality, are also a means of revenue to the craftsperson involved in making them.
5. Should this same result recur again, we shall be forced to cancel our subscription to your magazine.
6. The cashier picked up the can of soup, flicked it across the scanner and shoved it along the counter where it bumped up against a stack of other cans, such as, beans, tomato paste, frozen juice and canned fruit, but sometimes she had to punch a code number into the computer when it was a bag of fresh fruit or vegetables, such as, apples or celery, and the machine would beep three times at her if she made a mistake.
7. History is a subject that has always been of interest to me.
8. It was during the time that her brother was in high school that he was first introduced to the idea of making a career of wrestling.
9. He is an academic type of person.
10. My favourite day would consist of getting up late, eating breakfast and leaving the dishes for somebody else to do, sitting out on the lawn to tan, having an early lunch, lazing around for a while in the afternoon, maybe getting into the car and taking a cruise around town, or maybe having somebody drop in, having an early supper, watching some television and maybe taking in a movie followed by a bite to eat and bed.
11. This office needs someone to answer the telephone, answer or file the correspondence, type reports, and generally keep abreast of the office work.
12. After he had vacuumed all the rooms in the house, he dismantled the vacuum cleaner and returned it to its place in the closet in the hall.
13. Reading is a type of activity which allows readers to enjoy experiences that would ordinarily not be available to them in the normal course of events.
14. The Alsatian dog pricked its ears at the visitor as if wondering to itself why the visitor had come.
15. Putting your front tires on the back of the vehicle and the back tires on the front is a tried and true method of stretching the mileage out on your tires and keeping them in good shape without losing too much of the tread entirely or more on one side than the other.

Note that indefinite antecedent usage *must* be included in any discussion of wordiness. Refer to Grade 11, Indefinite Antecedent, pages 104 - 111, for additional exercises.

Chapter Fourteen

Grade 12

Writing Forcefully

Besides avoiding sentence errors and attempting good usage, one may take the following active steps to empower writing:

I. Produce Clear Transitions.

Inadequate transitions destroy the impact of a paragraph or an essay.

Each sentence must be clearly linked to the preceding sentence.
Each paragraph must be clearly linked to the preceding paragraph.

If a word or central idea appears at the end of the preceding sentence,
then *repeat or enlarge* upon it at the beginning of the following sentence.

The repetition or enlargement becomes **the hook** which binds the sentences together.

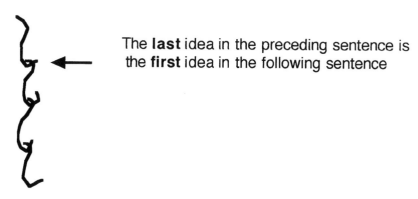

The **last** idea in the preceding sentence is the **first** idea in the following sentence

- Transitions in time order paragraphs:
  first, second, then, afterwards, next...

- Transitions in space order paragraphs:
  to the right, to the left, behind...

- Transitions in persuasive paragraphs:
  therefore, consequently, as a result, however ...

Example of transitions in time order paragraph:

• The *first* sign of activity in the kitchen was the sustained rattle of the tap water entering the tea-kettle. *Then* the opening of a cupboard door and the crackle of the plastic covering on the bread were *followed* closely by the clank of the toaster. Picturing the *activity* in the kitchen, Luke wondered if he should try to go back to sleep or follow his ears to the kitchen. *After* silent communion with his stomach, he decided on the *latter.*

Practice Exercise 1
Create clear transitions to link the following statements.
If necessary, change the order and add or delete words to clarify the meaning.

1. The dark water in the lake reflected the lowering clouds that were wind-blown and heavy with rain. Weedy spikes of grass fringed the lake. The level of water was low.

2. ... where for a little distance a rickety dock protruded into the water. Water oozed through the blackened boards and made the footing unstable. A small brown duck swam in circles.

3. Expansive willow trees grew to great heights because of their nearness to water. Their branches were canopies against the heat. Birch trees grew tall as well.

4. The grassy area in front of the cabins formed a natural amphitheatre. Flower beds brightened the view. The shape integrated the buildings, the lawns and the lake.

5. ... a hot drink. Chairs and sofas were filled with chilly individuals seeking warmth. Conversations trickled into a flood.

II. Be conscious of order.

A. Arrange items within a sentence or a paragraph in order of *increasing importance*. The effect is to increase emphasis or create suspense.

 • Dispirited, isolated and ill, she spent the day in her room.

 Note the added effect of alliteration.

B. Arrange items in *reverse order* for anticlimax or humour.

 • When he came to lunch, he was so nervous that he got the hiccups, upset his coffee, and used the wrong fork.

C. Ensure that the explanation made in subsequent sentences *follows the order* of the original statements.

> • *Sleeping or waking,* he was pursued by visions of the erupting aircraft. *Asleep,* he endured collages of flame and exploding machinery. *Awake,* his mind reproduced endlessly the tragic scene he had witnessed.

Practice Exercise 2
Rearrange the items in each sentence to achieve emphasis or anticlimax.

1. The dog, the horse, and the cat were equally aware of the change.
2. On Saturday Paul baked pies, made a list of chores, and cleaned the house.
3. A violent hurricane killed ninety people, levelled power lines, and interrupted airplane schedules.
4. Today was the worst day of my life: I failed a test, forgot to brush my teeth, and overslept.
5. This hair-style suits either male or female. The girl may wear the hair a little longer at the sides; the boy may want the back hair a little longer.

III. Avoid beginning a sentence with an introductory phrase containing the personal pronoun *it* or the adverb *there*. These words convey *no images*. They create *wordiness*. *Furthermore,* they are often accompanied by the verb *to be* which conveys *no action*. They cause the sentence to lose force.

> • *It was* late in the night that the storm broke.

> • *There is* a lane of towering poplars leading to the house.

Get rid of these words so that a definite image is presented immediately.

> • Late in the night the storm broke.

> • A lane of towering poplars leads to the house.

Practice Exercise 3
Rewrite each sentence forcefully.

1. There are several reasons why this statement is true.
2. It is unlikely that anyone will come at this hour.
3. There was a loud report from the front of the house.
4. It seems fair to ask a different person each time.
5. There used to be a spring of clear water on this site.

IV. Condense your sentence.

Replace clauses and phrases with fewer words or synonyms.

Reducing the number of words *while retaining the thought* concentrates impact.

Example 1:   • The house that is in the lane is up for sale.

Solution: • The house in the lane is up for sale.

Example 2:   • The tissue box, which is always well used, sits prominently at
                     the front of the room.

Solution: • The well-used tissue box sits prominently at the front of the
                     room.

At the same time **avoid ellipsis**, the improper removal of words essential to correct
   sentence structure.

Example: • The smaller pump works as fast or faster than the larger one.

Solution: • The smaller pump works as fast *as* or faster *than* the larger one.

                  ie., The smaller pump works as fast as (or faster than) the larger one.

                  Otherwise, the first sentence becomes "as fast than the larger one."

Practice Exercise 4
While retaining the content, condense the following sentences.

1. The type of rose that is a favourite with me is called *Night Star.*
2. He zigzagged to one side and then to the other in order to avoid the people walking on the road who were coming his way.
3. People who do not eat meat have to spend some thought on ensuring that their diet contains adequate protein.
4. She spoke in a quiet manner about her travels around the world and her adventures in many parts of it.
5. The tattered leaves on the aspen trees were a signal that fall was coming soon.

Practice Exercise 5
Avoid ellipsis.

1. She neither has nor will leave.
2. These plates are as old if not older than you are.
3. The gorillas were both interested and wary of Dian Fossey.
4. This pattern is both different and prettier than the other one.
5. Henry liked peanut butter more than his brothers.

V. Know the prime locations in a sentence.

A. Place an important idea at the end of a sentence so that its image is the *last one* to remain in the reader's mind.

- At the edge of the sand he spotted *a gleam of gold.*
- On Monday she tripped on the stair and *broke her leg.*
- At the beginning of the day he was *full of energy.*
- Across the lawn he noticed *a trail of garbage.*

Therefore, place prepositional phrases at the beginning of the sentence.
To show loss of impact, relocate the phrases in each example given above.

Although one cannot use this method all the time, *be aware* of the effect on your sentence of the location of prepositional phrases and adverbs of time, place and degree.

B. Particularly in a short sentence **the second important location** of a key idea is at the beginning.

- *One's initial response* is often correct.

C. Sandwich weaker words, such as, *also,* and parenthetical expressions, such as, *however, nevertheless,* and *on the other hand,* between the important ideas.

   • He was, *nevertheless,* afraid of no one.

The word *also,* particularly at the beginning of the sentence, creates an afterthought.

Solution: • He was *also* friendly.   **(Not** Also he was friendly.)

Practice Exercise 6
Rewrite these sentences to increase emphasis.

1. The writer is interested in finding a publisher, of course.
2. He will succeed without a doubt.
3. Also the payment must be made on the thirtieth of each month.
4. He backed into a concrete pillar while parking the car.
5. The first day of school is an exciting event to a small child.
6. He must come soon surely.
7. Lack of participation is the problem.
8. Coffee is a stimulant for some people.
9. The dolphin follows the boat, however.
10. The chairperson acknowledges that the price of seats has risen despite an active promotional campaign.

VI. Strengthen an idea by repeating it.

   • He was *never* late for school, *never* late for meals, *never* late for an appointment, and *never* late for a fight.

However, **remove** *unpleasant repetitions of sound.*

Examples: • The singers sang the song sweetly as parents smiled.

             • The ring of the grinding pin rang in the van.

Practice Exercise 7
Use repetition to increase the impact of these sentences.

1. He read frequently.
2. She was polite.
3. He liked flowers.
4. She slept most of the time.
5. He often laughed.

VII. On occasion write balanced sentences.

Balanced sentences are a mixture of *parallelism* and *repetition*.
They give the sentence rhythm.

- An excess of water is misery; a lack of water is death.

Practice Exercise 8
Write 5 balanced sentences on such themes as the following:

1. War and peace.
2. Want and plenty.
3. Leisure and work.
4. Nuts and bolts.
5. Hamburger and pizza.

VIII. Vary the type of sentence.

A. In a **natural order** sentence the subject is placed at the beginning.

- The *staple gun* fired a volley at the placards.

B. In a **split order** sentence the subject is placed near the middle. It "splits" the sentence.

- Hurrying around the hall, a *score* of workers dragged chairs into rows.

C. In an **inverted order** sentence the subject is placed at or near the end.

> • Away from the scene *he* fled.

Practice Exercise 9
Change the order of each sentence. *Is the impact greater or less? Why?*

1. The girl smiled self-consciously into the camera.
2. The noise carried from the eight loudspeakers for several blocks.
3. The firecrackers sizzled and crackled hundreds of feet in the night sky.
4. Through the congested streets darted the dog.
5. He spat a great volume of tobacco juice into the air.

D. A long sentence allows the development of rhythm and images.

> • Despite warnings against making a public protest, the group distributed pamphlets, launched rallies and organized marches in an effort to maintain momentum against the repressive and powerful regime.

E. A short sentence provides shock or finality. It may create closure to a longer sentence that precedes it.

> • The plan worked.

F. In a *loose sentence* the main thought is expressed early in the sentence. The sentence may be terminated at many points.

> • The car backed into the garage,▌slammed into an ancient garbage can, ▌knocking it down and ruining its symmetry forever, ▌jammed a fender against a modest work bench ▌that was covered with a neat array of tools, ▌and shuddered to a stop ▌against the substantial rear wall.

G. In a *periodic sentence,* details build to the central idea located at the end.

- At the very top of the ladder, which leaned giddily on one leg against the dusty wall and the rungs of which were mere suggestions of footrests, crouched an unusual and atavistic visitor, one which hadn't needed the rungs to make his way to his lofty perch - a truculent *barn owl.*

Practice Exercise 10
Identify each sentence as loose or periodic.
Rewrite in the alternative order. Indicate your preference.

1. The dance was a success because the band was excellent, the decorations were colourful, the prizes were innovative, and the crowd was cheerful.
2. Following the second intermission and before some of the early-nighters began to drift away, to everyone's astonishment appeared on stage a most surprising vocalist - a normally reticent student.
3. His baritone voice crafted the words of the ordinary song into poignant phrases that demanded attention and tugged at the heart.
4. He received a standing ovation when he had finished the tune, one that became the theme song for that year's graduating class.
5. At the very least, in the minds of his listeners had dawned the insight that tantalizes and surprises individuals throughout their lives - that people are not always as they seem.

H. Simple, compound and complex sentences allow variety.

- They fled the country.

- They caught the ferry *and* the boat became a refuge.

- They looked back fearfully at the land *which* they were leaving behind forever.

In a complex sentence **subordinate *the less important* idea.**

Practice Exercise 11
Subordinate the less important idea.

1. She arrived home where she found she was locked out.
2. While she shivered from cold, the wind blew.
3. They wanted a second helping of potato salad, since they asked for it.
4. The timers operated efficiently because the swimmers finished by noon.
5. The train braked as the car accelerated across the tracks.

I. **Words in apposition and participial phrases** create an interesting change from more common coordination and subordination.

- *A small white butterfly*, she circled gracefully among the party-goers who were chatting over teacups.

- *Sitting demurely on a chair that was much too large*, she surveyed the ebb and flow of exotic visitors.

Practice Exercise 12
Using words in apposition or participial phrases, combine these sentences.

1. The shoes sagged in heaps around the entrance. They looked down-at-heel and odorous.
2. He placed a finger on the first valve. Then he blew a resounding note.
3. The merchandise sported red sale tags. The merchandise was mostly imported goods.
4. An eraser is a most helpful piece of equipment. It is well used in the course of the editing process.
5. They thanked their host. They left promptly.

IX. **Use figures of speech**; such as, simile, metaphor, personification, alliteration, assonance, and onomatopoeia.

- Her face looks like a full moon.
- Her face is a full moon.
- The full moon leaned over a tree-top and glinted at me.
- The moon mirrored a sense of kindness and comfort.
- The river flows in sibilant hisses and bubbles around the wet rocks.
- Crack! went the gun; boom! went the drum; hooray! went the children.

*However, **avoid mixed metaphors**.*

- He broke the back of the problem because it tickled his fancy.

Practice Exercise 13

Use figures of speech to describe such ideas as sadness, joy, energy, grace, enthusiasm, fortitude, honesty, friendship, beauty, isolation, fear, and love.

X. For greater impact use direct speech.

Direct: • "Are you coming?" she called.

Indirect: • She called to ask if he were coming.

XI. Use concrete details to invigorate general statements.

Example: • Vine fruits grew well.

Amplified: • Grapes hung in heavy masses from sturdy, thriving vines.

Practice Exercise 14

Use concrete details to explain and amplify.

1. The room was crowded.
2. The building was empty.
3. The grandfather told stories to his granddaughter.
4. The snowfall was unexpected.
5. The race was close.

XII. Avoid trite expressions; such as, the following:

- few and far between
- depths of despair
- method in his madness
- clear as a bell
- chip off the old block
- cool as a cucumber
- calm before the storm
- dead as a doornail

XIII. Choose words that suit the subject matter.

A business letter or a report requires a different vocabulary from a descriptive or narrative essay. Denotative words may be more appropriate for the former; connotative words, for the latter.

Denotation refers to the *literal meaning* of a word.

- Diana left the room   *means*   Diana quit the room.

Connotation refers to the feelings and images evoked by a word.

- Diana flounced from the room.
- Diana staggered from the room.
- Diana raced from the room.
- Diana floated from the room.

Practice Exercise 15

Suggest connotations for the following groups of words.

1. proud, haughty, aloof, self-assured, supercilious, arrogant, poised.
2. flow, meander, trickle, inundate, ooze, percolate, slip.
3. lively, mischievous, energetic, playful, restless, intrusive, difficult.
4. smelly, pungent, acrid, redolent, aromatic, fetid, heady.
5. festival, brawl, carnival, party, fete, junket, jamboree.

Chapter Fifteen

Grade 12

Supplementary Exercises

I. Run-on Sentence
Use punctuation to correct the following sentences.

1. The gong sounds the lumberjacks heave themselves agilely up the poles when they reach the top they begin sawing furiously.
2. The 'super dogs' parade docilely after their trainers they appear unaware of the audience consequently they perform faultlessly.
3. Outside the house that is the lottery prize a line of stationary people snakes into the distance those waiting to see the interior gawk passively at the ones walking by and staring.
4. Tables in the Food Fair are congested as families test international cuisine others looking for a place to sit wander hopefully towards an empty chair is this one taken they ask.
5. A display of Chinese jade woven silk rugs and ancient artifacts gives an exotic air to one corner of a room noses press against glass cases for a closer look.
6. The horse barn envelops huge horses and small people a motley crowd of fathers mothers small and larger children eyes cautious they walk carefully along the cement runways behind the shiny rumps of equine leviathans.
7. Outdoors the sun is hot occasionally an exhausted walker sprawls in the shade of a building one or two sleep unaware of feet treading near them.
8. Coming around the corner of a building which displays Canadian arts and crafts stragglers are welcomed by a cheery brass quintet smartly uniformed performers that cause faces to lighten and tired hands to tap against pant legs.
9. As the day ages the midway activates the sky with circling lights neon signs and tinny tunes entice money from willing pockets others not so gullible avoid the garish compound.
10. The parking lot is still crowded however the prospect is less daunting since one is looking for a vehicle and not for an elusive parking-space there's the car one crams thankfully inside and drives away.

II. Sentence Fragment
Correct the following fragments by adding a subject and a verb or by attaching the fragment to the preceding sentence.

1. They shopped for bricks. For building a fireplace.
2. The rumble of the train was so loud that people waking suddenly in the night and trying confusedly to orient themselves.
3. After several attempts in the kitchen to remove the salt from salt water, the chief results of which were extensive puddles of dubious liquid on the stove, open cupboard doors, and far too many utensils cluttering the counters.
4. The announcement said, 'Three hundred years of collectibles for sale.' We rushed over. Three tables of tired plastic and mysterious tin.
5. Being sick has certain advantages. Except, perhaps, being told to rest completely instead of watching television.

6. If he says one more time that he never did things like this when he was a kid, and I should consider myself lucky to have a solid roof over my head and three good meals on the table.
7. Be really careful when you take out the ashes. Or, to put it another way, you will clean up the mess.
8. More and more companies are locating in already congested urban centres. A trend which may be illogical.
9. While traffic is becoming more noxious, drivers, more obnoxious.
10. They scattered from the place like flies. Just as expected.

III. Lack of Parallel Structure
Balance the structure in the following sentences.

1. Please enter your name and where you are presently living.
2. The article was produced, packed, delivered to the outlet and for sale.
3. The coach expects the team to come regularly to practice and that they will not slacken their commitment to the game.
4. The salesman approached not only the customers on the lot but also went into the street and encouraged passers-by to step inside for a look.
5. Seeing the bus approaching the toddler, she leapt into the street, grabbed him in her arms, and the child was saved.
6. She was a person of poise with many talents and friendly to all.
7. Having heard of her failing health and that she was unable to drive her car, the neighbours organized themselves to help.
8. He had worked at many jobs, at some for only a few months, for one or two years at others.
9. The play was well scripted, well acted and a thrill to watch.
10. If the problem is handled correctly, it will not only sort itself out but also it will be placed in its proper perspective.

IV. Misplaced Modifier
Correct the following sentences by placing single words or phrases beside the words which they modify.

1. Corey is home from the hospital after having his appendics removed to the delight of his colleagues.
2. She took over the business several years ago when her father died in an airplane crash and has done very well.
3. They only sold ten of the twenty cookbooks.
4. Winifred has her mother's height which she uses effectively on the basketball court.
5. When the student arrived at university for the first time in his life, he had to monitor his own work habits.

6. For several months she suffered from a nagging pain in her foot which has now largely disappeared.
7. The guests drifted out of the house as the sun rose and wandered to the beach for a swim.
8. A safari hat perched on his head in which stuck an assortment of fishing lures.
9. A set of Dickens' works was given to me by my parents at the age of thirteen.
10. They were pleasant people of large stature and friendly expression of varying age.

V. Dangling Participle
Place each participial phrase beside the noun or pronoun which it modifies.

1. When kept at room temperature, you will find the clay easy to handle.
2. We had difficulty parking, and before finding our seats Act One had commenced.
3. After asking for a small portion, my plate was heaped with potatoes and gravy.
4. Screen doors are generally used on porches, permitting the circulation of cool air and keeping out insects.
5. Having spent several years in prison for a crime he did not commit, the attorney-general ordered his release.
6. Approaching the customs barrier, it was decided that we would chance not being thoroughly searched.
7. Having been born with a gift for mimicry, the child's mother encouraged him to perform whenever relatives and friends ran out of conversation.
8. The costume was light, allowing her to caper with ease about the stage.
9. Having read the evening paper, the kitten was the next source of entertainment.
10. Swerving to the right, my front tire avoided the boulder.

VI. Lack of Agreement
Restore proper agreement to incorrect sentences.

1. A number of diners was standing in front of the door when the restaurant opened.
2. This cough syrup is one of the best that is sold without a prescription.
3. The uniform of the team, as well as of the cheer-leaders, have been designed by a local couturier.
4. Neither of the latecomers have a reasonable excuse.
5. Anyone is welcome to watch rehearsals if they make themselves inconspicuous.
6. The singers or the choir director are asked to provide the song titles to the adjudicator.
7. The arrival of several cars, thirty people of various nationalities, a band, and two half-ton trucks crammed with luggage and stereo equipment were enough to electrify the quiet town.
8. There is several businesses who have posted *Help Wanted* signs.
9. He is the only one of my acquaintances who have travelled extensively.
10. If one misses a train or a bus, you should make the best of it.

VII. Indefinite Antecedent

Correct indefinite antecedent reference.

1. The wood pile was located some distance from the house which made it a chore to refill the wood box.
2. The student did not have a pen. This limited his output.
3. On the news it said that the concert was sold out.
4. If you want to get a certain birthday present, write it on a slip of paper and give it to me.
5. Several buttons were missing from his shirt of which he seemed completely oblivious.
6. They decided on an alternative route. That was when the trip improved.
7. If fried food does not agree with the child, it should be baked.
8. My father was a tradesman, so this is what I want to do too.
9. The bank was dispensing counterfeit twenty dollar bills which was a real nuisance to honest crooks.
10. Sarah had her mother's smile which was always in place.

VIII. Incorrect Tense

Rewrite sentences in which tense is incorrect.

1. We should have liked to participate if there were room on the agenda.
2. The base camp expects to have had news of the climbers before sundown.
3. He does as he liked.
4. By the time the letter arrived, its news is common knowledge.
5. Before the sun rose, the crowds began to gather.
6. The story was always the same: Mick takes the car and Ben has to walk.
7. If she was competent, we would praise her.
8. He will leave promptly or I will call the police.
9. Newton's experiments demonstrated that gravity existed.
10. I would like a smaller size.

IX. Wordiness

Eliminate unnecessary words.

1. Her uncle is a rich man who is exceedingly affluent.
2. There were hundreds of people who were killed in the flood.
3. The movie ends up with the hero and heroine happily getting married.
4. The innovation introduced by the host of introducing someone from the audience who was watching the performance live turned out to be a hit.
5. The universal ambition of the entire school was to have a juke-box in one corner of the common area where all the students in the school congregated at lunch.

6. The adjudicators are unable to peruse your manuscript as the linguistics are ill-constructed, the punctuation is of debatable repute, and the vocabulary is abstruse in the extreme.
7. She laid the cloth on the table, collected an adequate number of utensils, placed the plates in their respective locations, set a glass in place for each diner and waited for the company to come.
8. She is a hard worker as far as her work goes.
9. Citizens of Mombasa never experience cold weather, and snow is unknown in that part of the world.
10. If it were not for the fact that you have a deep well, your water supply would be at risk.

X. Punctuation Review One
Punctuate correctly and give a reason in each case.

1. If you stand too long Henry you will be tired.
2. The dayliner a twenty-car train arrived on schedule.
3. Mountaineer James Evans successfully completed his climb.
4. Placing the package on the chair she left the room.
5. The group arrived not by car but on foot.
6. Into the deepest hole in the lake the canister plunged.
7. However that mystery was never unravelled.
8. The long hill which is directly to the left is a prehistoric barrow.
9. The crew departed early as a storm was forecast.
10. Place the dog on the leash and follow me.

XI. Punctuation Review Two
Punctuate correctly and give a reason in each case.

1. The daughter preferred cake the son pie.
2. Along the road sides of beef and pork collected flies.
3. Above the clouds the sun shone.
4. He constructs cabinets chairs tables etc in his basement workshop.
5. They swam and swam and swam.
6. Send the package please on February 11 1998 precisely.
7. The simpler question is the favourite the other is avoided.
8. The quilt was worked in tones of grey for example taupe charcoal and rhinoceros.
9. The snow lay only on the high slopes therefore skiing was restricted.
10. Put the following items in storage.

XII. Punctuation Review Three
Punctuate correctly and give a reason in each case.

1. The picnic a yearly event pleasantly occupied the community.
2. Holly bells and icicles these trappings are part of Christmas.
3. He rejected very rudely I thought her request for a donation.
4. Would you kindly move closer to the front.
5. The witness reported that she the defendant appeared composed.   (Editor's insert)
6. Ask the brother for spare tires chains and a wheel jack the sister for waterproof jackets
      blankets and hot soup and the daughter to monitor the telephone and relay messages.
7. The eagle returned although it was flying noticeably higher.
8. The buffalo or prairie bison is nearly extinct.
9. Samantha Jewell MA PhD is a distant relative.
10. Across the bay the clouds gathered.

XIII. Usage Review One
Correct improper usage.

1. He had several months holiday pay to collect.
2. Had you told us, we would of found some way to help.
3. They took my last cent off me.
4. As your leaving, collect your coats.
5. He wouldn't have done anything anyways; he doesn't like conflict.
6. That car was coming to fast to see the detour sign.
7. If its' food supply is decimated, it cannot survive.
8. Then she goes, "Have you heard the latest?"
9. Each week many people volunteer there time to community service.
10. The paint ran off of the wall and onto the rug.
11. He gave me alot of encouragement.
12. Loosing your way in a strange city is not unusual.
13. He was quite as soon as he was given his bottle.
14. Her principle ambition is to have her own business.
15. They seen so much violence that they became unstable.
16. My aunt was a strange women in a family of strange relatives.
17. By the end of the week, they get so bored of pasta.
18. She was too nice of a person to forget.
19. A souffle is kind of a difficult dish to make.
20. They were wondering where you were at.

XIV. Usage Review Two
Choose the correct form.

1. My sister is more agile than (I, me).
2. Everybody went to supper except (we, us).
3. The thief must have been (he, him).
4. They can swim as well as (she, her).
5. Football is a favourite sport with (we, us) Canadians.
6. For (who, whom) are you building the boat?
7. Who was it? It was (he, him).
8. Give the lighter loads to Karl and (I, me).
9. Gavin told (she, her) and (I, me) to enjoy ourselves.
10. (Who, whom) are you working for this summer?
11. Let the patient (lie, lay) quietly for a while.
12. That side pocket has never (lain, laid) flat.
13. The officer said to (lie, lay) down the keys so I (lay, laid) them down.
14. The dog was (lying, laying) asleep when the car drove into the yard.
15. He saw the presents (lying, laying) on the table.

XV. Usage Review Three
Correct improper usage.

1. Sit the monitor on this desk.
2. He acts like he has all the time in the world.
3. She seemed like she was interested.
4. This rabbit looks like it is friendly.
5. The children sat between the remains of the chocolate cake.
6. You are allowed a certain amount of practice swings.
7. The calculator makes less errors than my brain.
8. If you do real good at this job, your reputation will be made.
9. Our defence tries real hard, but there forwards are too strong.
10. Cigarette smoke has a bad affect on lungs.
11. The last time we argued was when you grew a beard.
12. This summer is certainly different than the last one.
13. The family was real pleased at him deciding to come home for Christmas.
14. Us leaving town so suddenly took all our friends by surprise.
15. You being selected was a compliment.

XVI. Usage Review Four
Correct improper usage.

1. Give any surplus stock to Peter, John, or myself.
2. Frances spending extra time on her music increased her confidence.
3. Them leaving school early was noted.
4. The leader has indicated that us four will introduce the panel.
5. Who do you think has the best chance? Lindsay or her?
6. Hand these umbrellas to whomever needs them.
7. He lead a debate on the issue of free trade.
8. This bag is not as heavy as I had anticipated.
9. The reason for the excitement is because he's a home town boy.
10. She's the one whose responsible for our success.
11. They asked us to not follow so closely behind the van.
12. The politician inferred that the country's ills were due to the previous government's mismanagement.
13. Due to declining enrolment this course has been cancelled.
14. This is the most slowest season for car sales.
15. Their continuous jokes over the past months have kept us laughing.

Note that students in Grade 12 are encouraged to review the material assigned to grades 8 to 11 and to rework the exercises.

Be aware of the nine major sentence errors and ways to avoid them.

XVII. The Last Hurrah

The adverbs *farther* and *further* tend to be used interchangeably.
However, *farther* may imply distance while *further* may imply depth.

- They walked farther on the last day of the trip.
- They went further into the topic.

Goodbye and good luck!

Works Consulted

For the material in this text I accessed three general sources: first, knowledge and skills which my elementary and secondary school teachers gave me when analysis of sentence structure and grammar were commonplace; second, early twentieth century texts on grammar and composition which I collected and enjoyed; and third, helpful books used during my teaching of secondary school English. The second and third sources I have listed below.

Buehler, Huber Gray, and Pelham Edgar. *A Modern English Grammar*. Toronto: Morang & Co. Limited, 1904.

Canadian Press Style Book. 1974.

Fowler, H.W. *A Dictionary of Modern English Usage*. London: Oxford University Press, 1949.

Irwin, H. W., and J.F. Every. *English Composition for High Schools*. Toronto: The Copp Clark Company, 1928.

Lang, S.E. *A Modern English Grammar*. Western Canada Series. Toronto: The Copp Clark Company, Limited, 1909.

Larock, Margaret H., Jacob C. Tressler, and Claude E. Lewis. *Mastering Effective English*. 4th ed. Toronto: Copp Clark Pitman, 1980.

Paton, J.M., and Allan D. Talbot. *The New Using Our Language*. Toronto: J.M. Dent & Sons, 1957.

Shaw, Harry. *Handbook of English*. 2nd Canadian ed. Toronto: McGraw-Hill Company of Canada Limited, 1970.

Stevenson, O.J. and H.W. Irwin. *High School English Composition*. Western Canada Series. Toronto: The Copp Clark Company, Limited, 1913.

Stevenson, O.J. and H.W. Kerfoot. *Ontario High School English Grammar*. Toronto: The Canada Publishing Company, Limited, 1929.

Strunk, William, Jr., and E.B. White. *The Elements of Style*. 3rd ed. New York: MacMillan Publishing Co. Inc., 1979.

Index for Part Five - Grade 12

Printed in the United States
by Baker & Taylor Publisher Services